FRANZ SCHUBERT

OCTET

for 2 Violins, Viola, Violoncello, Double Bass,
Clarinet, Horn and Bassoon
für 2 Violinen, Viola, Violoncello, Kontrabaß,
Klarinette, Horn und Fagott
F major/F-Dur/Fa majeur
D 803

Edited by/Herausgegeben von
Max Hochkofler

D1512800

Ernst Eulenburg Ltd

London · Mainz · New York · Paris · Tokyo · Zürich

I. Adagio – Allegro 1

II. Adagio 37

III. Allegro vivace 53

IV. Andante. 62

V. Menuetto. Allegretto 83

VI. Andante molto–Allegro 90

NOTICE

As in the 6th movement of the Octet there are some unusual difficulties for the 1st violin, several simplifications have penetrated into the performance practice. Unfortunately these alterations have got into almost all editions instead of the authentic reading (bars 124—130, 141—145, 325, 329—337, 348—352). Also the Clarinet part is simplified several times: While the alterations in the last movement are enforced by the simplified Violin part and thus may be excused, the deviations in the first movement (bars 33, 217) are thoroughly nonsense and anyhow should be rejected. Of course for our edition only Schubert's unfalsified text could be used. The autograph is preserved in the Vienna Staatsbibliothek.

The falsifications corrected in this score, are the following:

VORBEMERKUNG

Da das Oktett im VI.Satz der 1. Violine an einigen Stellen Schwierigkeiten ungewöhnlicher Art zumutet, haben sich in die Aufführungspraxis verschiedene Erleichterungen eingeschlichen. Bedauerlicherweise haben die Änderungen in fast alle Ausgaben Eingang gefunden und die authentische Lesart verdrängt (T. 124—130, 141—145, 325, 329—337, 348—352). Auch die Klarinettenstimme weist mehrere Vereinfachungen auf: während die Umänderung im letzten Satz (T. 323—324) durch den erleichterten Violinpart erzwungen und darum bis zu einem gewissen Grade zu entschuldigen ist, sind die Abweichungen im 1. Satz (T. 33, 217) vollkommen sinnlos und auf jeden Fall zu verwerfen. Für diese Ausgabe konnte selbstverständlich nur der unverfälschte Schubertsche Text in Frage kommen. Das Originalmanuskript ist erhalten und befindet sich in der Wiener Staatsbibliothek.

Max Hochkofler

Die in dieser Partitur beseitigten Verfälschungen lauten:

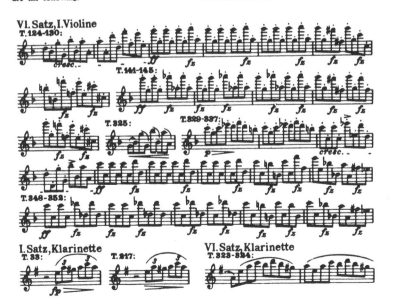

chromaticism —

Octet

I

Franz Schubert, Op.166
1797-1828

leaping octaves & scales

Relatus MINOR
D
2nd Subject
50

8

E. E. 1160

Db major recalls 2nd Sub

14

125

130

E.E. 1160

F# minor moves ↑ + chromatically → tension

K.E. 1160

combining motifs possible whereas extended melody not possible

violin e cello (2nd subject)

E. E. 1166

E.E.1160

E. E. 1160

harmonisation cl+fg + cor → mead
little hymn tune

E.E.1140

22

hanging G 8 bars borrowed

E.E. 1160

Same sub B♭ - subdominant

E.E.1160

H.K. 1160

B.E.1150

CODA— summing up in TONIC

E.E.1160

K K 1160

Serenade: B♭ subdominant - extended, long melodies / duets

II

F maj ← B♭ (SD) / C (D) / D minor - 6

37

Adagio

E. E. 11 60

42

E.E.1160

48

E. E. 1160

espectalton formal stately dance? nearer to händler
1 in bar: simplicity of motif

F MAJ   9. Pas

III   Minuet

Allegro vivace

block
change
tone
colour

E. E. 1160

M → C

54

E. E. 1560

Cma

key notes d ♭d F ♯♭b   distance key
D♭ mar

Flattened Submediant

55 ✻

40

Cl.(B)   pp

Fg.

Cor.(F)

unison passage not aware of harmonic progress.

Vl.   ff   fz   fz   fz   ff >   p   pp

Va.   ff   fz   fz   fz   ff >   p   pp

Vc.   ff   fz   fz   fz   ff >   p   pp

Cb.   ff   fz   fz   fz   ff >   p   pp

imitating horn call   bagpipes - rustic sound   D♭

50

Cl.(B)

Fg.   pp

Cor.(F)

Vl.

Va.

Vc.

Cb.

E. E. 1160

✻ becomes popular contrast / progression
Elgar - Nimrod   E♭ maj - key 3rd apart

56

58

different ways of harmonizing   descending motif

60

E.E.1160

E.E.1160

Allegro vivace da capo

Thematic variation – not good at motivic writing
cross rhythm & triplets

62

melodic: cannot deconstruct **IV** ∴ problem

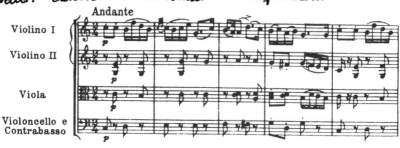

66

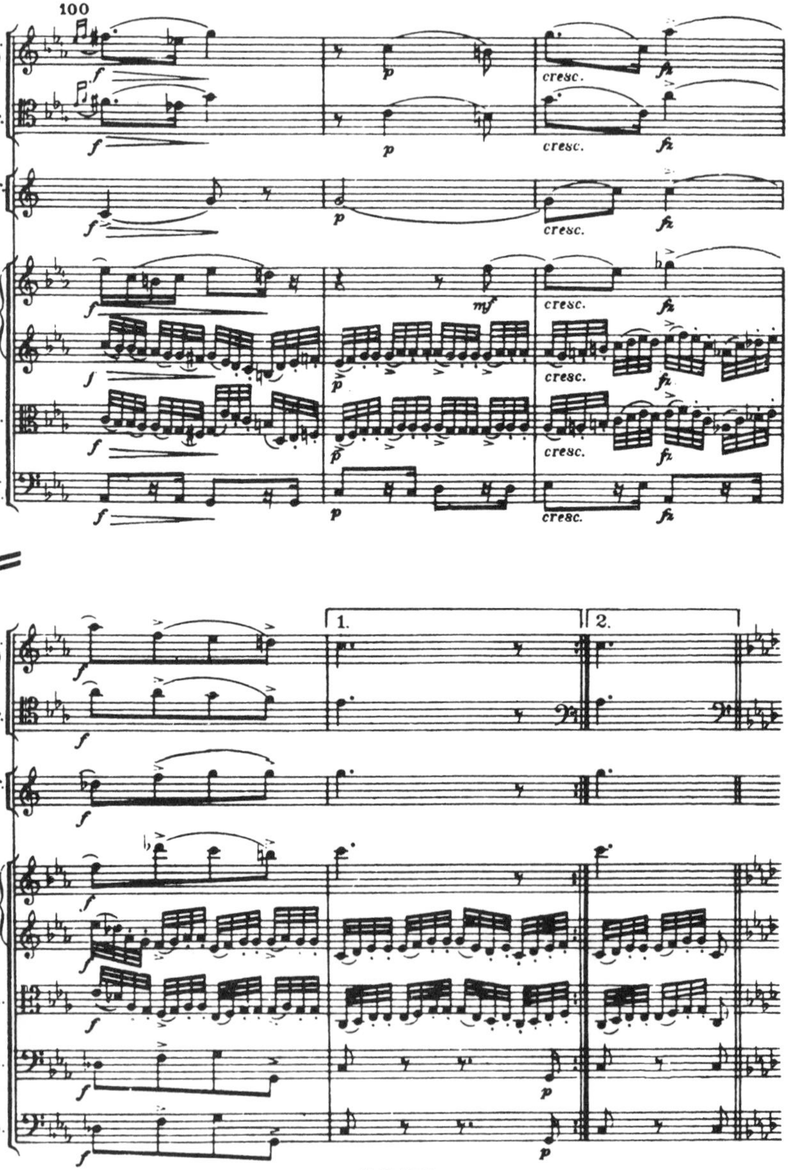
100
Cl. (C)
Fg.
Cor. (C)
Vl.
Va.
Vc. Cb.
cresc.
Cl. (C)
Fg.
Cor. (C)
Vl.
Va.
Vc.
Cb.
1.
2.

Var. VI

E.E. 1150

Var. VII.
Un poco più mosso

E.E.1160

Più lento *minor*

160
Cl. (C)
Fg.
Cor. (C)
Vl.
Va.
Vc.
Cb.
Cl. (C)
Fg.
Cor. (C)
Vl.
Va.
Vc.
Cb.
dim.
dim. pp
dim.
dim.
dim.
dim.
dim.
dim.

antiphony { strings / wind   expected speed, stately

sb

V

Menuetto
Allegretto

Ⓐ
Clarinetto in B
Bassoon. Fagotto
HORN Corno in F
Violino I
Violino II
Viola
Violoncello
Contrabasso
Double Bassoon.

little bit of Ino

10

Cl. (B)
Fg.
Cor. (F)
Vl.
Va.
Vc.
Cb.

E.E.1140

Cma

clarinet has countermelody in violins.

F ma

86

TUNE

Subdominant Eb major.   TRANSPOSES 1 note ↓   [Café music]

Bassoon

like B's ⅥII Minuet & Trio motivic, less bel canto

E.E.1160

E.E. 1160

harmonic sequence V^b I V^b I V^b I
melodic feature — suspension

Menuetto da cupo e poi la Coda

= Minuet Repeat

high & difficult from past — tension, on the edge
unworldly TIMBRE (see OU HG.)

f minor

double dotted notes also Ⓑ

VI

Andante molto

change of mood - tremeloes

M. K. 1160

wild changes of volume - poetry + music
~ MELODRAMA

WALKING BASS also Ⓑ Ⅳ

HOMOPHONIC } not counterpoint
CHORDAL

etc

classical 2 - 4 - 8 bars long
here 3 - bar phrase

94

E.E. 1160

C

90

2nd Subject
C major in dominant
light & merry

E.E.1160

100

E.E. 1160

Ab 2nd Sub

R.E.1160

triplets, more movement
texture increasing

fz = forzando – strongly accentuated (= sf)

2nd SUBJECT A MAJ.

106

E.E.1160

E.E.1160

= Recapitulation 1st Sub in F major

290

Recapitulation 2ⁿᵈ Sub
in TONIC

M pregnant pauses

300

E.E.1160

traditional for both 1ˢᵗ & 2ⁿᵈ Subject
in TONIC to finish dialogue

Unit 20/B

116

118

Revisits: violins - creepy

CODA— happy

Allegro molto

E. E. 1760

Song. The Doppelganger: Inner self: Jekyll & Hyde
aesthetics of Romanticism
esp. German= earth/ country images – HEIMAT

122

124